28

of
Resilience

VIVIENNE EDGECOMBE

To all of us who sometimes think our resilience might be at risk.

CONTENTS

ACKNOWLEDGEMENTS

Thanks to Jack for the love and the dinners, and for being my biggest fan.

And to Chantal for your clarity and consistency, and for all your support.

INTRODUCTION

This little book came into being from an audio series I created based on what I had seen about the nature of human resilience and what that means for us as human beings navigating our lives.

My intention is to provide 'bite-sized' chunks that you can reflect on, noticing what seems true to you and what questions you may have as you continue through each day's offering.

Feel free to give yourself the gift of time as you read this book; it's not something we do very often in our busy lives, and if you need an excuse to sit down and relax with a cup of something delicious, then I'm very happy to provide it for you!

I hope you enjoy the 28 Days experience, and I look forward to hearing from some of you about what you may hear, see or feel differently along the way.

DAY ONE

WELCOME, AND THANK YOU SO MUCH FOR JOINING ME.

I thought it would be helpful to set a context for the next 28 days of exploration, and I'm going to start by sharing what this is not:

- ~ It's not about giving you coping strategies

- ~ It's not about strengthening a resilience muscle

- ~ It's not about adding things to your personal development toolkit

My intention in this book is that what I share here, when you start to really see it (in a 'got-it-in-my-bones' kind of way), will take a load off your mind rather than giving you anything else to do.

It's about the power of understanding.

I'm going to help you, as best I can, to *understand* what resilience is, and point out to you the implications of that understanding.

So that's where we're headed!

First up, I have a new definition of resilience to share with you, to use as a springboard for the rest of our exploration.

My definition differs in a very significant way from the usual one about your ability to bounce back from adversity or difficult or challenging situations.

I define resilience as:

Understanding the **innate** capacity to return to clarity and mental equilibrium after having been in a state of mental stress or distress.

You may have noticed that my definition doesn't talk at all about circumstances; there's a very good reason for that, which we'll keep coming back to over the next 28 days.

As part of this exploration, I'll do my best to point you to why it's much more helpful to **understand** what's going on when you're not feeling resilient, than to attempt to cope or strategise your way out of those feelings.

We'll dive deeper into the truth: that the nature of resilience is the *nature of you*.

Because, you see, you are resilient *by nature*; you were born resilient, and it was not and cannot be removed from you by anyone or anything.

The deceptive nature of our psychological experience means we can lose sight of it, but we can't lose it. It's part of us; it IS us.

Resilience has shown itself to you every day, all your life, whether you saw it that way or not.

That moment when it feels like the sun has come out again after days of rain? Or when your head metaphorically pops back above the water after you've felt like you were drowning? The moment when you started to 'feel like yourself again' after feeling off-kilter or down?

That's the natural functioning of the human psychological experience, and we're going to explore that more over the next 27 days.

In the meantime, I invite you to think back over your life to those moments when you 'came back to yourself', and notice how that has happened naturally and repeatedly throughout your life.

DAY TWO

HOW CHANGE HAPPENS, WITHOUT EFFORT OR TRYING

I call what we're talking about today:

Realisation - the ordinary extraordinary

When I first started learning about the inside-out nature of life (the understanding I referred to on Day 1), people would talk about *insight* being the way we update our understanding of the world. And that seems true to me.

I see insight (or you could call it *realisation*), as the moment where my understanding of the way life works, or an aspect of that, becomes embodied - I get it in my bones, rather than just giving the automatic nod and thinking I get it on an intellectual level.

As an analogy, you could think of learning to ride a bike.

There is a moment when you realise something about balance and gravity and motion all together at once; not because you've intellectually decided to, but because something updated in your embodied understanding of how the world works. And once you know it, you can't un-know it, even if you get back up in your head and get the wobbles from time to time.

So, I started looking out for these mystical and magical things called insights that would transform my life. I tried to manifest realisations. I listened to everything I could; I tried to get into the feeling I had been told was the best one for attracting insights, and I waited. And sometimes they came, and sometimes they didn't.

What I understand now is that realisation is very ordinary.

Yes, it's *extraordinary* that we can see something new that we didn't see before. The way that new thought is delivered to us is, to me, mind-blowing and beyond the limits of what I can 'get my head around', but it is *the way the system works*.

It's as ordinary and extraordinary as gravity.

It works that way for all of us, and we've been having insights, realisations - new thoughts - since we were born.

We *realised* early on that our hand belonged to us, so we stopped punching ourselves in the face with it.

We *realised* that we could use our arms to pull ourselves up and steady ourselves as we learnt to walk.

We learnt to *walk*.

We 'got' how maths works.

We 'got' the symbols on the page represent words.

We are realisation machines, and that innate capability is not location, mood or feeling dependent. We will get a new thought when we get it, and that thought can change everything.

So, as we share these next 27 days, you can relax. There's no pressure to see, or get, or understand. You can read each day's offering once, or you can read it a hundred times. Whatever makes sense to you.

You're designed for new thought; you can rest assured that it will be delivered to you as you go through your life, just as it has been up until now.

It may not come in the package you were expecting, so if I have one recommendation, it's to set aside what you think you already know, and just allow yourself to relax in a state of curiosity and 'not yet knowing'. Comparing this understanding to what you already know is unlikely to help you see something new, and that's what this is all about.

So, until the next instalment, you may want to reflect on the times when you got new thinking about something, that helped you in your life.

Maybe you came to peace with a situation that was

bothering you; maybe you saw someone's behaviour in a new light; maybe you 'got' a thing you had been trying to get for ages. New thought is always available to us. We're never stuck with what we think.

Isn't that amazing?

DAY THREE

WHERE DOES RESILIENCE COME FROM?

On Day 1, I talked about how resilience is part of us and can't be touched; today I'm going to point as best I can to why that's true, and I'll do that by shining a light on where it comes from.

So where *does* resilience come from, and why am I so sure it's untouchable in us?

Well, let's get purely practical for a minute. It seems obvious and true to me that we are born resilient (if we need to put a label on it). Babies learn to navigate the world, falling over a million times while they learn to walk, burbling a lot before they learn to talk 'properly'; they don't hang on to mistakes and they don't beat themselves up about not getting it right the first time. They just seem to revel in the process of learning about the world around them.

Then, over time, we get innocently conditioned to start 'overthinking' our mistakes; we want to 'get it right' and we want the world to act in accordance with our wishes.

When things don't go according to those expectations, life seems hard to us, and we live in the feeling of that thinking about life. We feel like life is knocking us around, when in fact it's our thinking about life that's doing the knocking.

You see, we live in the feeling of our thinking, 100% of the time, not the feeling of whatever circumstances are playing out in our life. That's the essence of the inside-out understanding I referred to previously.

While some might feel initially that it's difficult to be up against our own thinking, in fact I find it very hopeful and here's why:

There's something *before* the thinking we have about life: *there's life itself.*

There's the energy that animates us; the pure potential that we are borne of and that beats our heart and heals our body until the moment we die.

It's *that* energy that allows us to even have the thoughts of resilience or non-resilience; the energy that allows us to have an experience of life at all. *That's* the energy that can't be touched or depleted; it's the nature of us, and the nature of resilience.

Scientists might call it the life energy, or life force – it's the same energy that opens a bud after the winter and that grows a plant. In Eastern philosophy, it's sometimes referred to as Qi; in the Southern Pacific, you'll hear it called mana. Cultures the world over recognize that there is an energy that powers living things, the absence of which leaves just a shell.

But while it's there, it's there, and there's nothing you can do to deplete it or diminish it. We can hurt our physical body, but there's no way of touching the energy that's powering us. The physical body can be injured or unwell; the energy that is the *essence of us*, remains until we die.

And that, my friends, is the key to resilience – knowing that there's something before our experience, creating that experience as it takes the form of Thought, and allowing us to be consciously aware that we're having it. Knowing that the energy of life is powering our experience, powering *us*, and that it will keep doing that until the day we die.

Tomorrow we'll talk about the psychological immune system, that puts this energy to use in a very practical way.

In the meantime, I'd invite you to just sit with this and let it settle – it's not often we stop to consider our connection to the energy of life and what it means about us.

DAY FOUR

THE PSYCHOLOGICAL IMMUNE SYSTEM

As I referred to yesterday, it puts the energy of life that's in all of us, to use in a very practical way.

It seems to me that we all take for granted the fact that we have a physical immune system. It seems natural to us (and of course it is) that when we cut ourselves, the cut heals without us 'doing it'. We just do our best to keep it clean and leave it alone. When we get a cold, we know that the symptoms are our immune system at work to rebalance the body and put the virus back in its place.

What's not so visible to us is that the mind has its own 'immune system' that is constantly resetting us to our default (peace of mind, love, contentment). These are the feelings people describe when they're feeling 'themselves'; they are the labels we give to what we experience in the absence of feelings we'd describe as taking us 'away from ourselves', such as anger, frustration, judgement or fear.

This 'immune system' (and of course, that's just a metaphor) looks to me like the outward manifestation of resilience - which I defined earlier as how we naturally regain mental and emotional clarity after having been caught up in a storm of thought.

I find it's easier to describe *how* we know we have this system at play, than to describe the system itself (it's made from the energy of life that runs through us, so it's pretty hard to pin down!)

We all know that a 'bad mood' doesn't last forever

We all know that even if we feel sad, we'll inevitably feel happy again (and vice versa)

We all know that if we feel nervous, we will relax again

Yet when we get these feelings we find uncomfortable, we tend to forget that *they're not permanent.*

We attempt to 'get rid of them' - to make ourselves feel better through techniques and strategies, and when sometimes those strategies seem to help, we try them again the next time we feel uncomfortable.

What we're missing, is that the only thing that changes how we feel is a change to our thinking, and that's a factor of our 'immune system' at work, not of anything we've done or haven't done.

The universal energy of life that we are all part of is the constant source of new, fresh thought that *always* brings about a change in feelings - we can rely on it.

When we think we are in charge of what we think, or that

we could influence it in some way, it makes sense to us to use strategies to change feelings of discomfort.

When we realise that those feelings of discomfort are simply a reflection of Thought (that same energy of life, taking form) bringing our experience to life in any moment, and will change naturally as Thought changes (and fresh thinking comes down the metaphorical pipeline), we are waking up to the existence of this psychological immune system.

Once we're clear that this system is always at play, we no longer need to cope with or manage our emotions - we can just let it be and enjoy the ride.

So, until tomorrow, maybe you'd like to experiment with that. What if you don't need to worry about feeling uncomfortable feelings, because you know they're simply a product of Thought, and never permanent?

Hmmmmm…

DAY FIVE

WHAT YOU CAN COUNT ON – YOUR CONNECTION TO LIFE

Hopefully over the last four days you may have started to see and feel that resilience is built in to the human operating system. It's part of you and part of life, and you can rely on it.

It's just the way life works.

We have our ups and our downs, and those ups and downs are completely normal and natural. We are human; we get to experience the entire range of emotions - that's the beauty of the design.

And when it seems like life is tough or you're at the end of your tether, it's helpful to remember that there's something beyond and before those thoughts of hopelessness - it's what's *bringing* you those thoughts, and it's what will bring you the ones that will carry a different feeling when they arrive. You'll notice I don't say *if* they arrive - it's a given that you will get new thinking, and with it, new feeling.

This is a constant.

This is just part and parcel of your connection to life, and it can be relied on.

You don't have to worry about how you feel in any given moment - that's just life doing its thing, giving you a felt experience of the energy of thought that's flowing through your mind and coming to life in your sensory system.

It's like the special effects team on a movie set – they make it look very real, but you can rest assured it's just the production team at work doing their job. Just as you don't have to hide behind the couch when a scary movie is playing on TV, you also don't need to worry about or be scared of what Thought has projected onto the screen of your mind.

Until tomorrow, you might like to just notice your feelings, and what's playing on the screen of your mind when you're experiencing them.

You may start to see that Thought and Feeling go hand-in-hand, regardless and independent of what's happening in your life.

DAY SIX

How do I build resilience?

If you've been with me so far, you might realise that this is a trick question.

Because, as we've been exploring over the last five days, resilience is what you're made of, so there's no need to build it. In fact, just as it can't be damaged or depleted, it also *can't* be built.

It's made of the infinite potential of the energy of life - why would we think we could add anything to that?

But in case you aren't quite seeing it yet, or feeling it in your bones, let me just ask you a couple of questions now, to remind you of and point you back to your own and others' resilience:

Can you remember a time, or times, that as you look back, you don't know how you got through, but you did?

Can you remember times when you surprised yourself with inner resources you didn't know you had?

Can you remember a time when people told you how brave you were and you didn't really see it as brave, you just saw it as doing what needed to be done?

And can you think of times when someone else has surprised you or you've been in awe of their resilience in a situation most would consider extremely challenging? I have some beautiful friends who inspire me and remind me every day of the resilient nature of human beings and the magnificence of the human spirit.

So, you can forget about building resilience; it can't be built and it doesn't need to be. It's the nature of you.

Until tomorrow, I invite you to look around you and notice it playing out throughout your life and the lives of those you love.

DAY SEVEN

"I'VE BEEN TOLD I HAVE TO MANAGE STRESS TO BUILD RESILIENCE - HOW DO I DO THAT?"

Oh look, another trick question!

Yesterday we established that resilience is built in and doesn't need to be built up.

If, as I'm saying, that is indeed true, then the belief that managing stress is the key to building resilience, or vice versa, is built on a very shaky foundation.

The fact is, like resilience, stress is vastly misunderstood, with terrible consequences for those who suffer from it. The relationship we have assumed between stress and resilience is not quite what we think it is.

Whereas it is assumed that those who are feeling stressed are experiencing symptoms of low resilience (or vice versa), that's not quite how it works. As we've been talking about so far, resilience isn't something that is conditional or which fluctuates – it's simply the nature of human beings.

Stress, on the other hand, is a symptom of misunderstanding where your feelings are coming from -

not a symptom of a lack of resilience. It couldn't be, because you *can't lack resilience.*

To put it another way, feelings of stress or anxiety are not telling you about your resilience levels; they're always, and only, telling you about the thinking you've got going on in any moment.

I see it in myself and I see it in others. When I'm thinking stressed-out thoughts, I get to feel the reflection of those thoughts throughout my mind and body. I might get a tight feeling across my chest and maybe a 'tension headache'. If I had a blood test at those times, it would likely show that I would have elevated levels of stress hormones running through my body.

When my thinking changes, my feelings change, and all those responses in my body to that stressful thinking change too. It's the way the system is designed.

But when we try to manage stress, we're misunderstanding what stress is, and adding to the mental load. We think our thoughts need to be changed, whereas in fact, when we see them as the wispy bits of vapour that they are, changing them seems irrelevant, and we can just carry on with our day, safe in the knowledge we're simply noticing our human experience playing out.

 All feelings are normal, and when we really see that they're all made of the same 'stuff' (the energy of Thought running through us and taking forms) they start to lose some of their power to scare us. This feels very different to me, and I hope my explanation is giving you a sense of that difference.

Let's take an example.

If I don't understand that my feelings are a reflection of my thinking, my internal monologue might go like this:

"I'm feeling anxious - what am I anxious about? What shall I do to fix it? I hate feeling anxious! I need to stop feeling anxious!!"

When I realise that my feelings are simply telling me about my thinking in this moment, here's what the monologue is more likely to sound and feel like.

"I'm feeling anxious. Huh. Must be thinking anxious thoughts right now. I wonder what we should have for dinner?"

Feel the difference? Between now and the next instalment, you might like to just notice where your thoughts have gone when you're feeling anxious or stressed. I can guarantee that if you're having those kinds of feelings, the thoughts you're having are not ones of peace, love and contentment.

The system works exactly as designed – for your feelings to mirror your thoughts.

DAY EIGHT

WHEN IT REALLY LOOKS LIKE A SITUATION IS CAUSING YOU TO FEEL A CERTAIN WAY, TAKE ANOTHER LOOK

You may have noticed that I've mentioned a couple of times that we're living in the feeling of our thinking, not of the circumstances we find ourselves in.

I thought this might be a good time to explore that a little further – make it a bit more explicit for you.

WHY SITUATIONS DON'T CARRY INHERENT FEELINGS

As I referred to earlier, something that's implicit in the inside-out understanding of life is understanding that Thought creates our moment-to-moment experience of life, and that therefore, situations don't carry inherent feelings.

In other words, there's nothing in a situation or another person that is capable of installing feelings into you. A situation does not possess qualities of happy, sad, joyful, tragic or any other feeling state.

This can be hard for us to get our heads around, as we've

been so conditioned to an 'outside-in' faulty view of life. In thinking that situations or other people or events can 'make us feel' any particular way, it seems to us that how we feel is inevitable given these circumstances.

It's a sad situation, so I must feel sad.

It's a happy circumstance so I must be thrilled.

But what if it's not always like that? What if I sometimes feel sad and sometimes happy and sometimes angry and sometimes peaceful, regardless of what's happening?

Or what if I 'should' feel happy (because the circumstances apparently have happy attached) but I don't? Or I 'should' be devastated, but actually I feel very peaceful?

Maybe, like me, you've experienced people telling you how you must feel in certain situations. We do it all the time, unconsciously. We project what we think *we* would feel, onto someone else.

We do it with the best intentions, to show empathy, but we don't have their thinking so, actually, we have no idea what they must be feeling. It's a best-guess that we assume is true, and we are often surprised or taken aback when someone expresses a different feeling from the one we had projected onto them.

Here are a couple of random examples I can think of,

where I've seen first-hand that people's experience varies wildly, yet we assume they will feel a certain way:

"Oh, you're moving house, you must be feeling stressed"

"Oh, you've been made redundant, you must be really upset"

"Oh, you're going to be have a baby, you must be thrilled!"

And what about when we have two or more different things going on, which supposedly have different qualities? One sad and one joyful?

Which one is meant to take precedence? What's the formula? Or are we meant to just feel semi-sad and semi-happy?

The more we look in this direction, the more it becomes clear that we feel happy when we are thinking happy, and we are sad when we are thinking sad. That's the determining factor, not the situation, event or person we have traditionally blamed or credited for our feeling state.

The (il-)logic of circumstances or other people dictating our feelings just doesn't stand up once we start to really look at it like this.

When we start to see that our psychological, or 'felt' experience of life is in fact generated entirely from the inside, out, via Thought, we can get a glimpse of the fact that those circumstances or other people are not what's causing our feelings of distress, upset, relief, happiness or joy. Thought is playing out in the theatre of our mind/body, and being projected outward at the world.

It looks like we're feeling the world, *but that doesn't make it true*.

We can believe the circumstances are dictating our feelings, but that doesn't mean they *are*.

Sometimes we have an experience that feels like our life has. been turned upside-down. For me, my experience of things like the unexpected death of a loved one, or facing decisions which felt like they had no 'win', had me thinking that those circumstances could be the exception to the 100% inside-out nature of life. *Surely* situations or events such as the untimely death of a loved one, a devastating earthquake leaving thousands homeless, or realising you can't have the children you wanted, have inherent qualities or just 'are' tragic or upsetting?

I'm certainly not saying anyone doesn't have a right to be upset, or should feel *any* particular way. All emotions are available and understandable in those situations, (as they are in any situation).

What I've seen though, is that it's not the circumstance itself which will determine your experience of it; what will determine your felt experience is entirely down to Thought running through you in any moment. That's why you can feel differently even when the situation is ongoing or unchanging - because your experience is not tied to the circumstance; it's tied to Thought.

I've witnessed people being flooded with feelings of peace in times when they had been experiencing great stress, even though nothing has changed on the outside.

I've seen people laughing when a moment ago they were crying. I've done it myself.

I've had other people *upset on my behalf*, when I've been perfectly peaceful about a situation or event.

I've seen and heard amazing stories of realising that although it looks like the outside world is what's scaring us, it's not; it's Thought that's scaring us – or more to the point, it's that we've lost sight of the fact that it's Thought that is creating this experience for us, not what we're thinking *about*.

That realisation is liberating and hopeful, because it releases us from the faulty cause-effect equation that keeps us trying to manage the outside world in an attempt to protect our inner feelings.

Our feelings were never at the mercy of the outside world, so we can relax and stop trying to manage it.

Until tomorrow, perhaps you'd like to reflect on those times when you 'thought' you were overreacting, or that you were surprisingly calm. And you can also reflect on those times when you thought someone else's reaction was over the top or that they seemed to be handling something much more calmly than you thought they would (or than you think *you* would)

DAY NINE

WHY ALL FEELINGS ARE NORMAL AND OK

As a result of the outside-in misunderstanding of life, we've been brought up to think that certain feelings are good and others are bad. Uncomfortable feelings are to be avoided or fixed at all costs, and replaced with 'good' ones at the earliest opportunity.

But what if that's not true? What if all feelings are just normal? We're designed to feel the whole range of emotions, after all. We're built for it. Our feelings go hand in hand with our thinking – that's the perfectly-functioning system that provides us with our felt experience of life.

Whether we are really aware of it or not, we have been conditioned to believe that our feelings are a reflection of what's happening in the world, or alternatively what happened in the past or what we think will happen in the future.

But if you really knew, in the moment of feeling the discomfort of an unwelcome feeling, that it was in fact the reflection of a *thought*, what would that do for you?

Have you ever seen a toddler have a tantrum, and then be laughing and giggling five minutes later? That's what happens when you don't get caught up in analysing and judging the feelings you have. They just play through you and you have the experience, and then your experience changes as your thoughts change.

The natural resilience that's built in shows itself in all its glory in the infinite possibilities of human experience.

It's completely normal to feel sad; we all have those feelings when we have sad thinking.

It's perfectly normal to feel angry. We all get to do that too, when we have angry thoughts.

It's perfectly normal to feel joy, despair, peace, frustration, hopelessness, hopefulness, distraction and presence.

It's perfectly normal.

It's the design of the human mind, and it's nothing to worry about.

You don't even have to take notice of those feelings if you don't want to. I know we've been taught that you have to chase down the root cause of the feeling so you can address it and move on, but you don't. That's entirely unnecessary, and it's a fool's game, because the root cause is right in front of us: we feel that way because we're thinking that way.

We'll feel differently when we get new thinking, which is

inevitable. End of story.

So, next time you find you're tempted to 'escape' a certain feeling, you can rest easy in the knowledge that a feeling can't hurt you, and all it's telling you is that you've got some thinking that feels like *that* at the moment.

Whew.

Until tomorrow, you may like to notice how, even when you're feeling a feeling you'd rather not feel, you're absolutely fine, anyway.

DAY TEN

RELAX, YOU DON'T HAVE TO THINK POSITIVE

As we've been exploring, Thought is what creates our experience of the world; the power of Thought is what gives us our good days, our bad days, our joy and our pain, our peace and our discontent.

So, doesn't it follow that we should try to 'think positive', and thereby hopefully have more of the good days, the joy and the peace?

Well, no.

If you've ever tried to 'think positive', you'll know that sometimes it seems like it works, sometimes it doesn't. If you genuinely see an upside to whatever's going on, you'll feel better. If you're trying to force it, it's not going to work, however much you tell yourself there's a silver lining.

Have you ever had someone say, "well at least (insert supposed upside of whatever's happening)"? Did that make you feel better, or did you want to slap them for being so insensitive?

Your reaction will depend entirely on what thinking

makes sense to you in that moment. You can't force yourself (or anyone else) to think a certain way.

To me, thinking positive often seems to imply that the situation is inherently negative, and that only by finding a silver lining or a 'better' way of thinking about it can we overcome that inherent negative nature.

For example, we try to convince ourselves with affirmations in the mirror of how confident we are (while the little voice in our head shrieks BS in the background) or we try to look on the bright side of something that seems to us to be truly upsetting.

However, once we start to see that the experience we're having of any situation is always and only the result of whatever thoughts we're having, creating our feelings in that moment, labels of positive and negative become somewhat irrelevant.

In the same way that the sand we use to build our sandcastles is not good sand or bad sand, it's just sand, and we can use it to create beautiful castles or scary sea monsters, the energy that is *Thought* is completely neutral – it's the shapes we make with it, innocently forgetting that they're creations of our own making, that scare us.

And in the same way that our sandcastles are washed away with the incoming tide, our thoughts are not permanent, and will dissolve of their own accord and be replaced with new thought when we forget to focus on

41

them.

So give yourself a break.

Rather than trying to find the bright side, you can just relax, and recognise that how you're feeling is simply a reflection of Thought, taking form in this moment, and this one, and this one.   Fresh thinking can come along at any time, inevitably bringing with it a different feeling from whatever you're experiencing right now.

You can rely on it.

Until tomorrow, why not play with this. Give yourself one less job to do, and see how it feels to know you don't have to think any differently from how you're thinking right now.

DAY ELEVEN

WHAT REALLY CAUSES STRESS?

What if the things we think stress us, are not the causes of our stress at all?

When I think of 'managing stress,' the image comes to mind of the arcade game I know as 'Whack-a-mole". You never know where the mole is going to pop up next, but you have to be ready to whack it back to where it came from.

Attempting to manage all the factors and circumstances of your life to minimise stress seems to me to be the same game - you just get one thing under control and something else comes up that you then have to manage in some way in order to not feel stressed.

Or else three of the little suckers come up at once and you've got no chance of getting them all.

And sometimes no matter how many times you hit the mole, it just sits there staring at you, and you have to accept it's not going anywhere.

If it were true that the 'moles' in our lives - circumstances and other people that we think are stressing us - really caused us to feel stress, we would either have stress nailed, or the situation would be completely hopeless.

Nailed - because if the stress were inherent in the circumstance, everyone would react the same, and stress would be predictable and quantifiable.

"Oh, Mr. Smith, I see you're moving house. You can expect a slightly elevated heart rate and sweaty palms for a period of three weeks or until the last box is unpacked."

Hopeless - because there are things we can never control or avoid, so we would all be doomed to a certain level of stress if those things happened - it's the absolute definition of being a victim of circumstance.

But that's not how it works, is it?

One person's stressor is another's 'meh' or cause for celebration. One navigates apparent adversity with grace and dignity, while another feels so much stress they end up with debilitating mental or physical health problems.

So here's the good news:

The stress isn't coming from the thing we're blaming for it; therefore, we are not, and can never be, victims of circumstance.

So if it's not my job, my family, my finances, my past or moving house, what is it then?

First, let's revisit how our human psychological system works.

Human beings are wired for experience. The energy of life is running through us - it animates the shell we inhabit and gives us our experience of our life through the form of thoughts. This Thought energy is constantly on the move, giving each of us a unique experience of our universe, from moment to moment.

Thought is the vehicle that gives us the full range of human experience - love, fear, joy, anger, stress, peace - all without us having to 'do' anything. Our thinking gives us an experience of all the human emotions as part of the natural flow of life.

What trips us up, is misunderstanding where the physical sensations of stress are coming from. And in fact, stress IS predictable; the predictor is where you think your feelings are coming from in any given moment.

When we're looking to something other than Thought as the cause of our stressful experience, we think that the 'thing' has to change for us to feel less stressed.

If that person would act differently, I would feel different (and by implication I can't if they don't)

If that hadn't happened, I wouldn't feel like this (and by implication I am doomed to feel like this for ever, because it did happen)

If that situation would change, I would feel less stressed (and by implication I can't feel less stress if it doesn't change)

If things don't or won't change, our mismatched expectations of how life should be and how it actually is, feed our stressful thinking, creating more stressful feelings.

Thought creates our feelings, 100% of the time.

This is the constant and reliable fact of how we experience any feeling, including feelings we label as stressful.

We don't have to factor any variables into this - it's just how the system works.

I'm not saying you shouldn't take care of practicalities in your life, or that you don't have too much work for one person to competently deal with in the amount of time you've got. I'm simply describing how the system actually works: in any situation or circumstance, what you're feeling is your thinking, 100% of the time, no exceptions.

So how's that helpful?

In the same way it's helpful to know how gravity works if you want to get water up a hill, and you've been using a rake until now, it's helpful to understand how the human psychological operating system works if you want to waste less time and energy doing stuff that doesn't make sense with the aim of feeling differently (i.e.: trying to manage stressors that aren't actually causing your stress).

Thought and its accompanying feelings are the weather on the sky of your being. You don't need to worry about it - it rains, the sun comes out, it rains again, and the sun comes out again. That's the system at work, and we don't (any more) feel the need to blame the weather on an angry god, or perform rituals to make it rain next Tuesday.

We know and accept that we're not in charge of the weather - it will just do what it does - but we do know that the sky is always there, whatever the weather.

We understand that the nature of nature is to flow, to keep moving; we just forget sometimes that we are nature and we are part of that flow of energy.

We forget that we're the sky.

Thought is constantly running through us; it's only when we forget that's just how it works, that our scary thoughts look real to us and we feel stuck. The moment we see our stressful feelings as part of Thought's natural creative power, they lose their scariness and their stickiness, and we can just get on with the job of living our lives, with all their ups and downs, sunshine and rain, moles and molehills.

Until tomorrow, let's go back to basics; just notice how your feelings follow your thoughts throughout the day. They go hand-in-hand and can't be separated.

They're two sides of the same coin; the energy that's bringing your experience to life.

When we're looking to something other than Thought as the cause of our stressful experience, we think that the 'thing' has to change for us to feel less stressed.

DAY TWELVE

"THAT'S ALL VERY WELL, BUT I DON'T LIKE FEELING STRESSED".

I'm not saying you should like it. I'm not telling you how you should feel - I'm just saying that this is how it occurs - from the inside, out - and that it's nothing to concern yourself with. Disliking a feeling doesn't change it - in fact, as we've been exploring, judging it is just adding another layer to it. It will just keep moving through if you stop going back and poking at it.

I'm not sure whether there's anyone out there who particularly enjoys feeling stressed (it's entirely possible there is), but I do know that you don't have to dwell on how you feel about your feelings. That's just another reflection of thought in action - thoughts about thought.

Oh, the magnificent creative power we have, to have thoughts and feelings, and then to have thoughts and feelings about our thoughts and feelings!

I find myself much more comfortable these days with feeling uncomfortable. I'm much less likely to go chasing the content of my thoughts to find out why I'm feeling like I am; I'm much more likely to carry on with my day and trust in the perfect design of the human operating system. When I look in that direction, I tend to notice that when I turn around a bit later, my feelings have changed, despite me.

So until tomorrow, how about testing it out? What happens when you don't concern yourself with how you're feeling, and just get on with your day?

DAY THIRTEEN

YOU'RE NOT UP AGAINST WHAT YOU THINK YOU'RE UP AGAINST; YOU'RE UP AGAINST WHAT YOU THINK

It's really built into our language: the mistaken idea that circumstances have inherent qualities that we are responding to, and that can affect our resilience in some way. For example, we say things like:

~ Life's hard

~ Change is scary

~ Marriage isn't easy

~ Relationships are hard work

~ Bullying damages people for ever

And at certain moments, with certain thinking, those things might look true to us.

But what about the moments when those things don't seem true?

When life doesn't look hard, and change seems exciting. When marriage feels like the easiest thing in the world and relationships are full of joy? When you look at the bully and see their pain and feel compassion, rather than taking it personally?

These counter-examples point to what we've been exploring throughout the last 11 days - the inside-out nature of our experience of life. Because we are so conditioned to think the power is in the circumstances, we take for granted that there are reasons (or excuses) for why it seems easier one day than it did the day before. Our reflex is to 'pin it on' something outside of us.

Maybe it's because I expected this change. Or it's because things are going better for me at the moment. It's because my husband is behaving himself right now. It's because my friends are all being kind. It's because I found out the bully had a tough childhood.

But actually, it's none of those things.

I'm not saying they're not true - I have no idea what's going on in your life. But I do know that your experience of life (of change, of marriage, of relationships, of bullying) will be whatever you think it is, in any moment.

And that's why, if we were to have a conversation about any of those circumstances, I would not be digging into what's going on out there - I'd be pointing you back to the role your thinking is playing in creating this experience in the first place (i.e.: 100% of it).

Until tomorrow, I'd love you to keep an eye out for exceptions. The times when life seems different from your usual 'take' on it. See if you can catch yourself in a generalisation that really doesn't always reflect your experience.

DAY FOURTEEN

WHY BOUNCING BACK IS A TRICK OF THE MIND

The subtitle of this book is "All you need to know about your innate ability to bounce back" and yet here I am saying it's a trick of the mind. What's that about?

Well, first, let me ask you something: do you think you have to bounce back when things go wrong?

What are you bouncing back from?

And what exactly is it that is doing the bouncing? Literally - what?

The idea that we have to 'bounce back' is tied to the faulty assumption that an event or circumstance could ever render us less resilient than we were prior to it happening.

In that false paradigm, it looks like we take a knock, and have to bounce back from it.

But it's not true, even if it seems that way.

The only thing you have to 'recover' from is being caught up in a misunderstanding of where your feelings are coming from; a storm of thought that looks like it's caused by whatever's going on for you.

Please don't think I'm minimising the importance of events that may have happened in your life. I know very well that life can deliver us things that most people would consider horrific or tragic.

What I see very clearly though, is that we will each have our own individual experience of those things, because we are each living in our own, Thought-created reality.

When you see clearly again how the system is working, what looked like 'bouncing back from adversity' becomes more about recognising what's really going on. There's nothing to work on.

Rather than bouncing back, you can pick up from a place of clearer understanding, and take the next step forward.

So *there's* the slight trick in the subtitle of this book. All you need to know, is that however serious the situation may seem, your experience of it comes to you via Thought, and it's Thought that will bring you a different experience of it at some point.

So until tomorrow, if you happen to experience a 'thought storm' notice how the storm changes in intensity and passes of its own accord. You may even notice that there are moments when you're ok with the storm, or forget about what you were upset about altogether.

DAY FIFTEEN

IT DOESN'T MATTER HOW YOU FEEL

Please don't think I'm being callous or uncaring. It's not that at all. I don't mean your feelings don't matter and therefore I can call you names and tell you all the things that I think are wrong with you, and you have no right to feel hurt or take it to heart. That's not it at all.

What I mean is, you don't have to be concerned about how you feel. And here's why.

How you feel is not telling you about the seriousness of the situation.

How you feel is not telling you about what the future will be like (your feelings have no idea what the future holds).

How you feel is not being transmitted to you from a future situation (your feelings don't live in the future, they're only right here, right now).

How you feel is not telling you about how nasty another person is, or how unfair life is (your feelings don't know about other people, or even life).

How you feel is not telling you about your choices or

your lack of choices (your feelings don't have any opinions about choice or lack of it).

How you feel is always, and only, telling you about the thinking you have happening in this moment. And this one, and this one.

And that's important and relevant when we're talking about resilience, because it relates directly to what we explored earlier - you have the energy of life running through you, giving you the ability to have this experience in the first place.

The forms that experience takes are drawn from a menu of infinite possibilities, so to attach any meaning to having a particular one seems a little 'out of perspective'. It's ALL the human experience, and once you start to see that your feelings are simply a reflection in any moment of thought playing in the movie theatre of your mind, the perspective shift happens of its own accord.

Your feelings are the special effects team of your thoughts. They seamlessly follow your thinking and, like all good special effects, you would never know they were made up. Once you start to see the production team at work behind the scenes, you can experience the effects without feeling at the mercy of them. It doesn't matter how you feel, when you understand where those feelings are coming from.

So until tomorrow, you might like to start to notice your

own 'special effects team' at work, and sit back in admiration at the incredible job they do of bringing your thoughts to life.

DAY SIXTEEN

WHY SELF-CONFIDENCE IS A RED HERRING

There's a whole industry built around selling you the idea that you are lacking in self-confidence, and that self-confidence is what it will take for you to achieve anything in life and become the resilient, successful person you've always dreamt of being.

I'm here to tell you, you can stop it. You can stop looking for self-confidence - it's a figment of your imagination. It's not something that can be built or destroyed, because it's a made-up construct of the human creative power of thought. Someone, once upon a time, had the idea that it was a good idea to believe in yourself, and that would make it easier to achieve what you want to achieve. Then someone else built a business around it.

Sometimes we get feelings of inadequacy and insecurity, based entirely on thoughts of inadequacy and insecurity. In those moments, it looks like we lack self-confidence. Sometimes we don't have that insecure thinking, and we feel capable and resourceful. In those moments, we think we have self-confidence.

If you are looking for self-confidence as a 'commodity',

you are doomed to disappointment: all human beings have moments of insecure thinking and feeling inadequate. That's normal.

When you see that self-confidence is simply a bunch of thoughts we've slapped a label on, it makes less sense and becomes less compelling to go searching for it or try to 'build' it.

But here's what's even more powerful: when you see that self-confidence or feelings of inadequacy or insecurity are brought to you by the power of Thought, and that Thought is simply the energy of life running through you and feeling like whatever you're calling 'lack of self-confidence', you are free to go and do whatever you need or want to do, *regardless of how you're feeling in any moment.*

It's not feelings of inadequacy or 'unresourcefulness' that are holding you back; you don't need to pay any attention to them. When you mistakenly believe they're telling you about your *actual* capability or resourcefulness, *that's* when you stop yourself from doing the things you want or need to do.

DAY SEVENTEEN

WHY STRESS ISN'T 'JUST PART OF THE JOB'

We're just over half way and I hope you're getting a sense of why resilience is a fact of life and the nature of the design.

Today we're going to explore why it's not true that we have to accept a certain level of stress with a certain job. Some people think their job is special, and has an inherent level of stress attached to it. That belief is perpetuated by society and comes at us from all directions. It's hardly surprising most people fall for the misunderstanding, when it's commonly and mistakenly accepted as true.

The truth is, there's no inherent stress in any job. If there were, everyone would feel stress of some form, all the time, when in one of those jobs. Instead, we see some people thriving, taking the workload or the nature of the work in their stride, feeling interested and curious about what the next day, week or month has in store. We see others seemingly drowning under the same workload and dreading coming to work the next day. We see the same person, feeling overloaded one day and resourceful the next, even though the workload or the type of work hasn't changed. *It's not the work*. It's their thinking about the work.

So that means stress isn't just 'part of the job' - it's not inevitable and it's not inherent to the type or volume of work you do. It's entirely a product of thought in each moment, and that's what you will have an experience of. You feel what you think, 100% of the time.

You may well have a workload that's too much for one person. That happens. However, your experience of that workload is entirely a product of your thinking in any moment. Stress is not your only option - it's just one from the infinite menu of human experiences that you could have in any moment, and could change at any time, when you get new thought.

So until tomorrow, I'd invite you to see if you can strip back to the facts. What I mean by that is, see if you can separate what you think is stressing you, from your thinking about it. This is about making your thinking visible to you, so you may even want to write it down, in a table of two columns: What's actually happening, and What I think about it. Make sure any assumptions about what it means for you or for other people sit in the 'Thought' column, even if you believe they are 100% correct!

DAY EIGHTEEN

WHY COPING MECHANISMS AREN'T REQUIRED

… and couldn't do a better job than the perfectly-functioning human operating system.

In the same way that 'managing stress' isn't required for resilience, nor are coping mechanisms or techniques to build or uncover your resilience. Once you know it's already and always there, even when you've lost sight of it, it makes less and less sense to try and find ways to 'cope' with uncomfortable feelings, or with feeling less than resilient.

Your mind is designed to thrive. It's designed to self-correct and go back to the default settings of peace, joy, presence, connection and love (or whatever labels we put on those feelings that are present when we're not caught up in insecure thinking).

But it's a hands-off system.

It does it without and despite our interference. Techniques or strategies to try and force a reset may look like they worked, which tempts us to try that again next time.

But what about when they don't work?

Actually, that's a trick question, because they never work, since it's never a technique which causes a change in our feeling state.

It's new thought, and that's coming down the line whether we like it or not, from wherever thought comes from. We're not in control of that, even when it looks like we are.

The system is designed perfectly, and it's working perfectly, giving us the felt experience of whatever we are thinking (whether we are conscious of our thoughts or not) at any moment.

You don't need to be concerned that you don't have the feelings you want to have, you can just let the self-correcting system do its thing. It's what it's meant to do, and it's what it will do whether you attempt interference or not.

I spent a lot of time blaming or crediting my shifts in thinking on techniques and strategies I had been taught. I disregarded the times they didn't work as me 'not doing it right', or not having found the 'core issue' that was keeping me stuck.

Once I realised that new thought was on a fool-proof delivery system, and would come whether I was ready or not, I quickly lost interest in going searching for the root 'thought', and lo and behold, my experience of life got much easier and more graceful.

When I lost interest (to a large extent) in the content of my thinking, and just noticed that I was in the experience of whatever thinking I am having, I was able to notice the system at play and just let it do its job. Even though it doesn't do it to my timetable, it's reassuring to me to know that it's working exactly as it's meant to.

So until tomorrow, I invite you to get much less interested in the content of whatever you're thinking, and look upstream – what's powering your thinking? What's thought made of?

What we think is nowhere near as important as the fact *that* we think.

DAY NINETEEN

WHAT OVERWHELM IS REALLY TELLING YOU

Everyone feels overwhelmed from time to time. That's natural and normal - you don't need to worry about it.

One of the teachers I learnt this understanding from used to say, 'so what'?

Our feelings feel really important when we think they're telling us about our situation, our plight or about the person in front of us. But when we see that all they're telling us about is the thinking we're having, it feels much more 'so, what'?

"So, what?" - I'll have another thought soon, which will bring a different feeling

"So, what?" - If I look to what's powering this experience of overwhelm, what's making it even possible, that puts my momentary feeling of overwhelm in perspective.

"So, what?" – this feeling is not telling me about the situation, it's just telling me I've got some 'overwhelm-flavoured' thinking going on.

This feels much lighter to me, when I see it. If it doesn't

feel that light to you or if it still looks serious and seems like the situation is 'doing it' to you, it's ok, it just means you haven't seen it yet, or you're not seeing it in this moment.

The moment you really see it, the suffering is gone.

So until tomorrow, you're welcome to question what any feelings of overwhelm might be telling you, and remember that they're simply telling you that you have that flavour of thinking going on.

And if you feel inspired to do so, you can even have your own "So what?" moment, and feel the difference for yourself.

DAY TWENTY

WHEN YOU THINK YOU'VE HIT ROCK BOTTOM, JUST STAND UP

There's an analogy I'd like to share with you, that to me, speaks directly to the innate resilience I've been pointing to throughout this book so far.

So, for now, just sit back, and relax, while I take you on a little storytelling journey...

Imagine, if you will, that you live in a swimming pool.

Everyone you know lives in the same swimming pool, and you're all skilled to different degrees at treading water to stay afloat.

Every now and then, someone comes along with a new tip to improve your water-treading technique – maybe you need to move your hands in a slightly different way, or sit up straighter in the water.

Each time, the treading water gets a little easier for a while, and then you notice that it's still really tiring and you're still treading water and looking for the next big breakthrough in water-treading technology.

Then one day, you see a couple of people floating past, looking completely effortless in their water treading – almost as if they were just walking. You think they must have something very special about them, or some unseen yet powerful equipment like a next-generation flotation device, or stilts, that would let them seem like their water-treading experience is so free of struggle. You catch their attention, to ask them about their secret.

They look at each other, and then look at you, with a compassionate chuckle.

"You're in the shallow end. Don't you realise you can just stand up?"

Now, you're a little taken aback, and bit skeptical of this advice – you've been in this swimming pool your whole life and no one has ever told you that you're in the shallow end. You've only ever seen people struggling to keep treading water.

But you can see that these people are having a much different experience, so you decide you'll try it. You put your feet down and lo and behold, you are, indeed, in the shallow end. Everything becomes easier and more graceful, and life feels less like a struggle.

Sometimes you forget, and end up treading water again, but before long you remember where you are and you just stand up again.

You wonder why you were never told this before – it's such a relief.

That's what I've been pointing to during this exploration over the last 18 days.

You are always in the shallow end.

You have the energy of life running through you, that can't be touched or broken or depleted. The only thing that gets in the way of you seeing that at any moment, is your understanding of how life works; your understanding of where your feelings are coming from.

When you see that you're just caught up in a thought storm, you are more likely to look back upstream to the amazing life energy, the power source that brings those thoughts to life in you and without which you wouldn't be having any experience at all.

If you could see that, what would it matter what thoughts you were having? What would it matter how you felt in any particular moment?

Why struggle with the outputs of that Thought energy, when you can simply see that it IS Thought and that it's not something you control or 'do'.

Whatever's served up to you in this moment, will not be what is served up next. You are simply feeling the reflection of your thinking – that's all you need to know.

When you see that, your feet are already on the ground.

Until tomorrow, you might like to think back to times when you stopped treading water and just stood up. They may have disguised themselves as moments of "I surrender" or "I'm sick of fighting this feeling", or "I don't have to feel this way".

There will be more than you think.

DAY TWENTY-ONE

THE IMPLICATIONS OF MISUNDERSTANDING

As I pointed to in yesterday's analogy about treading water, there are implications to misunderstanding how life works. In general, life feels harder and we feel 'done to', more of the time.

Today I'd like to take a look at the things people do to try and feel better when they're misunderstanding where their feelings of stress, overwhelm or distress are coming from.

When we think we need coping strategies to deal with stress, rather than realising that we are naturally resilient, people turn to what makes sense for them - what they *think* allows them to escape from the feelings they're finding uncomfortable.

For some that might be yoga, exercise, meditation or walking in the woods. They have mistakenly attributed their feelings of wellbeing to those things – they've given them credit for helping clear their mind or making them feel better.

That's not how it works, but that's how it looks to people – it's how it looks to all of us at least some of the time.

For others, the habit they have attributed their escape from painful thoughts to, can be more physically harmful - consuming alcohol or drugs, binge eating, self-harming or other 'addictions'.

When we think our feelings are coming from our circumstances, and we feel like we can't change our circumstances, it makes sense to us that our feelings aren't going to change, so we need to overcome or escape them in some way.

The person who does meditation or goes running for 2 hours every day to try and achieve peace of mind is doing exactly the same thing as the person who drinks too much to numb the feelings they're finding so uncomfortable – they're looking to something outside of them to try and find peace of mind.

When we're caught up in this misunderstanding, we hit a problem; sometimes we don't have access to the thing or activity we think our wellbeing, peace of mind or clarity is dependent on. If we can't drop everything and meditate, or do yoga, or go for a run, or have a glass of wine, what do we do then? Are we doomed to just stay feeling the way we're feeling?

Luckily, it's simply not the case that our clarity, wellbeing or peace of mind relies on any of those things. You don't have to look outside you for something that is what you're made of.

I'm not saying you shouldn't meditate or exercise, or drink alcohol either for that matter. People will do what makes sense to them. Me too.

But I know for sure, that when I really understand that my feelings aren't caused by what I am pinning them on, it doesn't make sense to do those things *in order to* achieve peace of mind. That's not where peace of mind comes from.

Peace of mind is what's already there when we see beyond the thought storm. Peace of mind is what's there before Thought.

There's no distress before Thought.

And when you see that Thought is made of the same energy that you are made from, there's no need to be afraid of it. You don't have to be afraid of what you think. You can just think it, and feel it, and move on.

So until tomorrow, I invite you to take a look at the things, situations or people you attribute your wellbeing or peace of mind to. What or who is it you have mistakenly thought until now, gave you peace of mind or joy, 'cleared your head' or 'calmed you down'?

What would it mean to you, and for your life, to know that your wellbeing and peace of mind are not dependent on those things or people, and are available to you at any moment?

DAY TWENTY-TWO

THE IMPLICATIONS OF UNDERSTANDING

Just as yesterday we saw that there are implications to not yet understanding the nature of our experience, and how our mental life is being created through Thought, there are, of course, implications to understanding.

If you saw your thoughts and feelings as the energy they are made from - sand you've built some scary sandcastles with - what would that do for how you relate to how you feel?

For me, when I see it (and I don't always see it), it takes away the sting. One thought becomes like any other. They're all made of the same stuff, after all.

"Oh, here's the 'I'm so stupid' thought again"

Oh, here's the 'my partner is driving me mad' thought again

"Oh here's the I can't handle this thought again"

"Oh here's the I need a drink thought again"

"Oh here's the I have to do two hours of exercise or I'll

go mad" thought again

In a Ted Talk by Michael Neill, he describes the moment he realised his thoughts of suicide were just that - thought - and that they weren't instructions or commands. He didn't need to act on them, no matter how compelling they seemed. In his words – "oh, here's the suicide thought again".

Thoughts are all made of the same stuff. It might seem like a big stretch, but *realising this could change your life.* "I can't handle this" is made of exactly the same stuff as "what's for lunch?".

Until we pile the rest of our judgements and assessments and fearful thinking on top of them, they're simply thoughts, little wisps of energy that would float through if you didn't pay them any attention. And when you see that, it becomes much clearer which ones are worth paying attention to.

So until tomorrow, you might like to ask yourself what's left when you strip away the judgement, fear or criticism from a thought you've been finding troublesome or scary. I'd love to hear what you find out.

DAY TWENTY-THREE

WE'RE ALL THE SAME

Today I'd like to ask a question, and then do my best to provide you with an answer that could be helpful in your life.

The question is this (put a couple of different ways):

Do you think there's something wrong with you? That you're less resilient than other people? That others are better at life than you?

If you answered yes to any of those, here's what I'd love you to know:

There's nothing wrong with you.

You have the same inner source of strength and resilience as everyone else.

Everyone is just doing what makes sense to them, given how they see the world at any point in time. Including you. Including me. We're all just looking for a little bit of peace of mind, we just don't always realise it's within us; we can't find it out there in the world of coping strategies or habits or rituals.

When we stop looking out there, when we see that everything we need is right here, then we see past the content of the thoughts and feelings we're not enjoying, past what's being created to what's doing the creating - this life energy that we're all made of, that's beating our heart and healing our wounds and breathing us without our input or interference - and we can know that we are all the same, in the ways that matter.

Thoughts will come and go, feelings will come and go (they will) and the energy of life will continue to animate us and give us an experience of this beautiful, mad, glorious, crazy, desperate, hopeful, magnificent life.

You're fine. I'm fine. We're all human beings riding the rollercoaster of Thought and feeling that is how we experience life. The more we see that that's just how we work, the less terrifying the ride!

Until tomorrow, I'd love for you to see what you notice about the energy of life and what it's doing for you without requiring your input or attention.

DAY TWENTY-FOUR

THE MOMENT OF CHANGE

Today we're circling back around to realisation, as we get towards the end of our 28 days. I wanted to revisit this, in case you might be thinking that you hadn't seen what you wanted to see yet about Resilience.

I want to reassure you that however you see the world in this moment is completely normal and understandable based on what you're thinking and feeling in this moment. That's how we work. And here's another reminder about how change really happens, so that when it does (and it will), you'll understand what's taken place.

You see, there's a moment in life that changes things.

It's the moment that evolves us, that sets us on a new path, that lets us move forward. It's the moment of realisation, of seeing something new.

It's the moment change happens.

We tend to think of change as a process – we're taught that it takes time, and that there are 'phases' to go through.

In fact, change is a moment.

It's the moment when we see something in a way we didn't see it before. We get a new thought, and that thought makes sense to us. It becomes our 'new point of view' and inevitably means different behaviours and different results.

In fact, it's the only thing that can result in those things.

We've been conditioned to think that things outside us are responsible for changes to our behaviour (if he wasn't so annoying, I wouldn't have to snap at him) or our feelings (if the targets weren't so high I wouldn't feel so demotivated) when in fact it's not possible for those things to have any control over how we behave or feel.

That's an inside job, brought to us courtesy of the power of Thought.

Thought is what creates our feelings, and when we believe what we're thinking, our behaviour necessarily follows, 100% of the time.

How many times have you acted in a way that seemed like a good idea at the time, only to look back later and wonder "what was I thinking?". It happens to all of us, because we all change our minds when a new thought makes more sense to us than the old one.

A change of Thought (you might call it a realisation, an

insight, or new thought) is what leads to changes in our feelings and therefore our behaviour, nothing else.

You see examples of this throughout the human life cycle:

The moment when a baby realises they have some control over their hands and arms

The moment when a child finds balance on a bike

The moment when a person comes to peace with the death of a loved one

The moment when someone truly decides to stop smoking or drinking

I remember, as a university student, skipping some particular classes. I'm sure I made up lots of reasons why I did that, and it doesn't really matter now.

I very clearly remember realising, however, that if I wanted to get through this degree and get decent marks, I would need to go to all or most of the classes, and put effort into completing the assigned work.

You'd think that was obvious and common sense, and of course it is. I'm sure I'd even thought it before, but until that moment, I had other thinking that looked more compelling and real to me. I suspect I was trying to avoid the discomfort I was feeling when I thought about not being very good at those subjects – proper head-in-the-sand stuff! But until I really saw something new, that was the behaviour that made sense to me.

Once I had new thinking about it, it made more sense to go to the classes and do the work, which of course led to vastly improved results.

This is a universal experience. We all work like this. So if you're feeling less than resilient, or you've got a habit of thought you know isn't really helpful but you can't seem to change, this is why. And you can relax - you'll see it when you see it. New thought is on its way, and who knows what shape it will take or what timetable it will follow. But keep looking in this direction. You will see these moments of change happening in all areas of your life.

Until tomorrow, you might like to take a look at the areas of life where you feel stuck, or where you know you have some unhelpful habits or behaviours that you can't seem to shift. Do they look like habits of thought to you?

If not, take another look; it's all they can ever be.

DAY TWENTY-FIVE

WHAT DOES NATURE SHOW US ABOUT RESILIENCE?

Let's take a wee step back, as we start to draw this little book to a close.

First, I have one of those quite profound questions for you:

Do you know that you are nature?

We talk about nature as if it is something separate from us. There are human beings, and then there's nature. There's us, and there's that.

We forget that we are nature. We forget that we are, each of us, the result of thousands of years of evolution and random miracles - what are the chances that you were born? Just look at the chances that yours were the sperm and egg that met that fateful day, let alone the fact that that randomness stretches back generations upon generations. Whether from a scientific or spiritual perspective, you really are a miracle of nature.

And what does this nature that we're part of show us about resilience?

Does the cycle of the seasons not show us, year in, year out, about the resilience of nature?

Does the regeneration of the land after the devastation of a forest fire not demonstrate the resilience of nature?

Do we not see in the way nature fills in the gaps and grows things in deserts, how strong and resilient nature is?

So, when we see the truth of ourselves as nature, can we not see that we too have risen, we too keep going, we too have seasons and cycles and ups and downs. But we're part of nature, and nature is strong and resilient, by nature.

Until tomorrow, you might like to consider the resilience of nature and how it is reflected in us all. What examples can you find in your own life that show the truth of this?

DAY TWENTY-SIX

WHY I'M NOT WORRIED ABOUT YOU, AND YOU DON'T NEED TO BE EITHER

Do you have a friend who's not scared of you?

If that seems like an odd question, let me explain...

Sometimes we don't tell people how we're feeling, because we don't want them to worry about us or feel like we're putting our 'load' onto someone else.

We sort and filter what we tell, to which friends or family members, based on what we think they can 'handle'. We don't want to burden them with our 'stuff'. We don't want to worry them. It feels heavy to us and we don't want to lay it on them.

The thing is, you can't 'lay it on me'. When a person understands that they can't feel someone else's emotions or experience - that we're each living in the feeling of our own thinking, not anyone else's - it's natural that they aren't scared about the strength of your feelings, and can just be there in support.

That's what I mean by 'a friend who's not scared of you'.

When you know for a fact that a person is ok, that they're just in the middle of a thought-storm, even when a situation seems serious, it's impossible to feel burdened or overwhelmed by what's going on for them. You can have compassion for their suffering, but not join them there.

Do you have a friend, or someone you can talk to, who you know isn't scared of your worries and fears, or your overwhelm, no matter how serious it looks to you?

I feel very lucky to have several of those people in my life, for when I've momentarily lost sight of it for myself. They're the ones who just love me and gently point me back to the truth - that I'm fine, and that this is simply the human experience in action.

They're the ones I call on at those times, because I know they won't buy into my stories of doom or my drama. They're not scared of my temporary feelings of upset or overwhelm, and there's something very reassuring in that.

And having some understanding of the inside-out nature of life lets me be that person for them in return, and for my clients and anyone else I end up in conversation with. And that's what it will do for you, too.

Until tomorrow, you might like to think about who this is for you – the person who doesn't jump headlong into your drama with you, whose very presence you find reassuring because they show you a different experience is possible.

DAY TWENTY-SEVEN

WHAT DOES THIS ALL MEAN FOR YOU?

It's day 27 of our 28 days, so it's time to start bringing all this together.

Over the last 26 days, we've explored what resilience is, where it comes from, what gets in the way of us realising our own resilience in any moment, and the nature of our human experience.

So what does it all mean for you? Maybe you've seen something for yourself over this time that speaks to that in a way that's tailored for you. Or maybe you're still just staying curious and noticing what you notice as you go about your life. Either way, it's great to be here with you as we look to what's true about how we work as human beings.

Here's some of what I see, about what it means for me and for you, to know that we have resilience as part of our make-up; that it's what we're made of rather than something we have to try to find or build.

It means we can rely on it.

We can take it for granted, in the same way we take

gravity for granted. Even on the days or in the moments that we feel like we've lost it, there's something very reassuring in knowing that it's there anyway. In the same way that we don't worry the sun has disappeared for ever, or that we have to go looking for it, once it sets at night, we can rest assured that resilience hasn't gone anywhere - we have just lost sight of it for a moment.

And that means that all the mental effort you thought you had to expend on 'strengthening your resilience muscle' or 'overcoming negative thinking' is redundant. You can put those things to one side - you are resilient by nature, not because you worked on it from birth.

So until tomorrow, if you happen to have a moment where you feel like you've lost sight of your resilience, I invite you to remember that even if you can't see it or feel it, it's always there, and you don't have to go looking for it.

DAY TWENTY-EIGHT

SO HERE WE ARE! DAY 28

I've loved having you with me for this little foray into the nature of resilience and the nature of you and me.

Whatever you've heard or seen is fine, and whatever questions you still have are fine too – it's normal that there are places in our lives where we see this more clearly than in others.

So a few parting thoughts and reflective questions on resilience, just to let you sink into it one more time…

Resilience is what you're made of. How would it feel to know that in your bones?

What would it do for you if you really see that?

Resilience is what everyone else is made of too.

What does knowing that in your bones change about how you are with someone you love who may be finding life hard at the moment? How is it helpful to know they're fine, they're just caught in a storm of thought, and their peace of mind and resilience is there, waiting for the storm to pass, as it inevitably does?

You may have already seen, heard or felt something about these implications of understanding as we've gone through the 28 days. And if something's hovering just in the corner of your eye, you can feel free to read this little book over and over again, if that's what makes sense for you.

I have loved sharing this with you, and pointing you as best as I can with the words I've got, to the truth of the magnificence and the miracle of human resilience.

And until we speak again, I'd like to leave you with this parting thought.

You have everything you need, already within you, to navigate this rollercoaster of a life. All the resilience, all the clarity, all the peace of mind you could ever look for is right there within you – it's part of you, it's what you're made of.

You can stop looking for it out there, and just rest, assured that it's built in to the design of you.

Thanks so much for being with me over the last 28 days – I wish you so much love for your onward journey.

If you'd like to continue the conversation, you can find resources and other options in the pages that follow.

Take care

Vivienne

HOW TO CONTINUE THE CONVERSATION

Here are some suggestions if you'd like to continue this exploration.

Visit my author website
http://www.vivienneedgecombe.com/

Here you will find resources, news about new and upcoming books and online courses, and options for taking a deeper dive into the inside-out understanding with me.

If you're interested in organisational change and employee wellbeing, you might like to visit my other website: http://www.insideoutchange.co/

Contact me by email:

transform@insideoutchange.co

RECOMMENDED READING:

I recommend any of the books and audios by Sydney Banks, to whom we owe a huge debt of gratitude for his articulation of what he saw at such a deep level about the human experience.

For those interested in exploring the Inside-Out understanding in a business context, I also recommend Instant Motivation by my colleague Chantal Burns.

ABOUT THE AUTHOR

Vivienne lives and works in the beautiful French Pyrenees mountains, with her husband, a dog, a cat and some chickens. Once upon a time, she said "I want to go to France and write a book". And somehow, that's exactly what has happened.

Vivienne shares the inside-out understanding with people from all walks of life who would like to experience more peace of mind and clarity in their lives, through her writing and coaching.

http://www.vivienneedgecombe.com/

Printed in Great Britain
by Amazon